VEGAN COOKBOOK FOR BEGINNERS

DELICIOUS AND VIBRANT RECIPES FOR A HEALTHY LIFESTYLE

-THE BAKE PUBLISHING-

The Bake Publishing

TABLE OF CONTENTS:

CHAPTER 1: VEGAN RECIPES 7

- VEGAN CESNECKA 8
- VEGAN ZUCCHINI BROWNIES 10
- VEGAN TUNA SALAD 12
- HOMEMADE SLOW COOKER VEGAN CHILI 14
- VEGAN STIR-FRY NOODLES 17
- VEGAN ENCHILADA BAKE 19
- VEGAN PIZZA MARGHERITA 21
- SIMPLE VEGAN GARLICKY POTATOES 26
- JACKFRUIT VEGAN TACOS 28
- VEGAN MUESLI 30
- VEGAN GRAVY 32
- VEGAN POTATOES AU GRATIN 34
- VEGAN QUINOA AND GUAC BOWL 37
- VEGAN STEW 40
- VEGAN FRENCH ONION SOUP 42
- VEGAN SPRING ROLLS 44
- VEGAN MUSHROOM AND KALE SOUP 47
- VEGAN COCONUT CURRY WITH TOFU 50
- VEGAN PUMPKIN BREAD 52
- VEGAN SWEET AND SOUR MEATBALLS 55
- PROTEIN-PACKED VEGAN PANCAKES 58
- VEGAN BAKED POLENTA WITH RADICCHIO 60
- VEGAN APPLE DUMPLINGS 63
- GRILLABLE VEGAN BURGER 66
- VEGAN LASAGNA 70
- VEGAN CURRIED CAULIFLOWER, SWEET POTATO, AND LENTIL SOUP ... 73
- VEGAN ITALIAN VEGETABLE SOUP 76
- VEGAN SWEET POTATO CHICKPEA CURRY 78
- VEGAN BURRITOS 80
- VEGAN PUMPKIN COOKIES 84
- VEGAN PORTOBELLO STROGANOFF 86
- VEGAN MUSHROOM RISOTTO 89
- EASY VEGAN WAFFLES 92

QUICK VEGAN EGGPLANT PASTA	94
VEGAN CHOCOLATE PIE	96
VEGAN SEITAN CURRY WITH RICE	98
VEGAN BLUEBERRY MUFFINS WITH APPLESAUCE	101
VEGAN AFRICAN STEW	103
VEGAN PUMPKIN PIE	105
ORANGE VEGAN CAKE	107
VEGAN DILLY RANCH	109

© Copyright 2021 by Clean Eating Publishing All rights reserved.

The following Book is reproduced below with the goal of providing information that is as accurate and reliable as possible. Regardless, purchasing this Book can be seen as consent to the fact that both the publisher and the author of this book are in no way experts on the topics discussed within and that any recommendations or suggestions that are made herein are for entertainment purposes only.

Professionals should be consulted as needed prior to undertaking any of the action endorsed herein.

This declaration is deemed fair and valid by both the American Bar Association and the Committee of Publishers Association and is legally binding throughout the United States. Furthermore, the transmission, duplication, or reproduction of any of the following work including specific information will be considered an illegal act irrespective of if it is done electronically or in print.

This extends to creating a secondary or tertiary copy of the work or a recorded copy and is only allowed with the express written consent from the Publisher. All additional right reserved.

The information in the following pages is broadly
considered a truthful and accurate account of facts and as such,
any inattention, use, or misuse of the information in question
by the reader will render any resulting actions solely under their purview.
There are no scenarios in which the publisher or the original author of this work can be in any fashion deemed liable for any hardship or damages that may befall them after undertaking information described herein.

Additionally, the information in the
following pages is intended only for informational purposes
and should thus be thought of as universal. As befitting its nature,
it is presented without assurance regarding its prolonged
validity or interim quality. Trademarks that are mentioned are done without written consent and can in no way be considered an endorsement
from the trademark holder.

CHAPTER 1: VEGAN RECIPES

VEGAN CESNECKA

Prep:
15 mins
Cook:
25 mins

INGREDIENTS:

2 tablespoons vegan margarine (such as Earth Balance®)
1 small onion, chopped
6 cloves garlic, crushed, or more to taste
1 tablespoon caraway seeds
1 teaspoon salt, or to taste
½ teaspoon ground black pepper
5 cups water
1 tablespoon vegetarian chicken-flavored bouillon granules
3 potatoes, diced

Croutons:

2 slices bread, cubed, or more as needed
1 tablespoon vegan margarine
salt and ground black pepper to taste
1 pinch oregano, or to taste
1 pinch onion powder, or to taste
1 pinch garlic powder, or to taste

DIRECTIONS:

1

Heat margarine in a medium-sized pot over medium heat. Add onion and garlic and cook until onion is soft
and translucent, 3 to 5 minutes.
Add caraway seeds, salt,
and pepper and cook for another minute.
 Add water and mix in bouillon. Bring soup to a boil, about 5 minutes. Add potatoes, adjusting water as needed to cover potatoes by a few inches. Reduce heat to a simmer and cook until potatoes are soft, but not mushy, 15 to 20 minutes.

2

Meanwhile, toss cubed bread in a pan with margarine over medium heat. Sprinkle salt, pepper, oregano, onion powder, and garlic powder on top. Cook, shaking the pan occasionally to cook evenly, until crouton are crisped, about 10 minutes.

NUTRITION FACTS:

239 calories; protein 5.1g; carbohydrates 38.9g; fat 7.6g; sodium 813.2mg.

VEGAN ZUCCHINI BROWNIES

Prep:
15 mins
Cook:
25 mins
Additional:
5 mins
Total:
45 mins

INGREDIENTS:

cooking spray
1 cup white sugar
½ cup brown sugar
½ cup olive oil
1 tablespoon vanilla extract
2 cups all-purpose flour
½ cup cocoa powder
1 ½ teaspoons baking soda
1 teaspoon salt
3 cups shredded zucchini
1 cup vegan chocolate chips

DIRECTIONS:

1

Preheat the oven to 350 degrees F (175 degrees C). Spray a 9-inch square pan with cooking spray.

2

Combine sugar, brown sugar, and olive oil in a large bowl; beat with an electric mixer until well combined. Mix in vanilla extract. Add flour, cocoa powder, baking soda, and salt and mix until combined. (Mixture will be dry).

3

Add zucchini and mix with a spoon until incorporated. Allow to sit for 5 minutes until mixture becomes more wet. Stir in vegan chocolate chips. Transfer batter to the prepared pan.

4

Bake in the preheated oven until top is dry and edges have started to pull away from the sides of the pan, 25 to 30 minutes. Let cool completely before slicing.

NUTRITION FACTS:

246 calories; protein 2.9g; carbohydrates 37.8g; fat 10.6g; sodium 269mg.

VEGAN TUNA SALAD

Prep:
10 mins
Total:
10 mins
Servings:
8
Yield:
8 servings

INGREDIENTS:

½ cup olive oil
¼ cup soy milk
1 teaspoon sea salt
1 teaspoon white sugar
1 teaspoon Dijon mustard
1 teaspoon rice vinegar
1 cup drained canned chickpeas (garbanzo beans)
½ cup chopped dill pickles
1 stalk celery
¼ cup dried chopped onion
1 teaspoon dried dill weed

DIRECTIONS:

1

Blend olive oil and soy milk together in a blender until thickened. Add salt, sugar, and mustard; turn on blender and drizzle vinegar through the opening in the lid until mixture is smooth. Add chickpeas, pickles, celery, onion, and dill; blend until mixture is evenly chopped.

NUTRITION FACTS:

171 calories; protein 2g; carbohydrates 10g; fat 14g; sodium 448.7mg.

HOMEMADE SLOW COOKER VEGAN CHILI

Prep:
25 mins
Cook:
4 hrs 10 mins
Total:
4 hrs 35 mins
Servings:
8
Yield:
8 servings

INGREDIENTS:

1 tablespoon olive oil
3 bell peppers, chopped
2 onions, chopped
4 cloves garlic, chopped
1 zucchini, chopped
1 yellow squash, chopped
1 cup chopped fresh spinach
2 (28 ounce) cans diced tomatoes
1 (15 ounce) can whole kernel corn, drained
1 (15 ounce) can black beans, rinsed and drained

1 (15 ounce) can kidney beans, rinsed and drained
1 (15 ounce) can garbanzo beans, rinsed and drained
1 (12 ounce) can tomato paste
1 cup vegetable broth
6 tablespoons chili powder
1 tablespoon dried oregano
1 tablespoon ground cumin
salt and ground black pepper to taste

DIRECTIONS:

1

Heat oil in a large skillet over medium heat; stir in bell peppers and onions. Cook and stir until the onion has softened and turned translucent, about 5 minutes. Add garlic and cook until fragrant, 1 to 2 minutes. Transfer to a slow cooker.

2

Add zucchini, yellow squash, and spinach to the slow cooker; stir to combine. Mix in diced tomatoes, corn, black beans, kidney beans, garbanzo beans, tomato paste, vegetable broth, chili powder, oregano, and cumin. Season with salt and pepper.

3

Cook on Low for 4 to 5 hours.

NUTRITION FACTS:

337 calories; protein 15.4g; carbohydrates 63.5g; fat 4.7g;

VEGAN STIR-FRY NOODLES

Prep:
20 mins
Cook:
15 mins
Total:
35 mins
Servings:
2
Yield:
2 servings

INGREDIENTS:

½ (8 ounce) package dried soba noodles
1 tablespoon oil, or as needed
¼ cup onion
2 cloves garlic, finely chopped
1 cup assorted mushrooms
¼ cup chopped eggplant
6 leaves bok choy, chopped
2 tablespoons soy sauce
1 teaspoon teriyaki sauce
ground black pepper to taste

1 teaspoon sesame oil

1 green onion, finely chopped

DIRECTIONS:

1

Bring a large pot of lightly salted water to a boil. Cook soba in boiling water, stirring occasionally,
until noodles are tender yet firm to the bite,
5 to 6 minutes. Drain.

2

Heat oil in a large skillet over medium heat. Add onion and garlic and stir-fry for 1 minute. Toss in mushrooms and eggplant; cook for 2 minutes more. Add cooked soba noodles, bok choy, soy sauce, teriyaki sauce, and pepper. Cook until bok choy is tender, about 2 minutes.

3

Sprinkle sesame oil and green onion over vegetables and serve.

NUTRITION FACTS:

326 calories; protein 12.2g; carbohydrates 53g; fat 10g;

VEGAN ENCHILADA BAKE

Prep:
15 mins
Cook:
45 mins
Total:
60 mins
Servings:
6
Yield:
1 casserole

INGREDIENTS:

1 cup crushed tomatoes
2 cups cooked white rice
1 (15 ounce) can vegetarian refried beans
½ (16 ounce) can diced tomatoes and green chiles
8 ounces sliced seitan
½ (8 ounce) package shredded mozzarella-style vegan cheese
9 (6 inch) corn tortillas
1 (15 ounce) can green enchilada sauce

DIRECTIONS:

1

Preheat the oven to 350 degrees F (175 degrees C).

2

Pour crushed tomatoes into the bottom of a casserole dish. Layer 1/3 of the rice, 1/3 of the beans, 1/3 of the diced tomatoes, 1/3 of the seitan, 1/3 of the vegan cheese, 1/3 of the tortillas, and 1/3 of the enchilada sauce into the dish, in that order. Repeat with 2 more layers.

3

Bake in the preheated oven until vegan cheese melts and casserole is heated through, about 45 minutes.

NUTRITION FACTS:

395 calories; protein 21.9g; carbohydrates 57.5g; fat 8.4g;

VEGAN PIZZA MARGHERITA

Prep:
20 mins
Cook:
1 hr 8 mins
Additional:
15 mins
Total:
1 hr 43 mins
Servings:
4
Yield:
4 servings

INGREDIENTS:

Pizza Crust:

¼ cup water
3 tablespoons flaxseed meal
5 cups cauliflower florets
½ cup rolled oats
1 teaspoon dried rosemary
½ teaspoon salt
¼ teaspoon garlic powder

Vegan Mozzarella Cheese:

¾ cup cashews

1 ¼ cups water

2 tablespoons tapioca starch

1 tablespoon nutritional yeast

1 teaspoon apple cider vinegar

½ teaspoon salt

¼ teaspoon garlic powder

Marinara Sauce:

1 tablespoon olive oil

6 cloves garlic, finely chopped

1 (14 ounce) can crushed tomatoes

2 tablespoons balsamic vinegar

1 teaspoon maple syrup

1 teaspoon salt

1 teaspoon red pepper flakes

1 teaspoon dried oregano

½ teaspoon ground black pepper

Toppings:

½ cup cherry tomatoes, sliced

½ cup basil leaves

DIRECTIONS:

1

Preheat the oven to 450 degrees F (230 degrees C). Line a baking sheet with parchment paper.

2

Whisk 1/4 cup water and flaxseed meal together in a large bowl. Let sit for 5 minutes.

3

Place a steamer insert into a saucepan and fill with water to just below the bottom of the steamer. Bring water to a boil. Add cauliflower, cover, and steam until fall-apart tender, 3 to 6 minutes. Let cool, at least 10 minutes.

4

Grind oats, rosemary, 1/2 teaspoon salt, and 1/4 teaspoon garlic powder together in a food processor until flourlike in texture.

5

Place cooled cauliflower in a fine cheesecloth and squeeze out as much moisture as possible.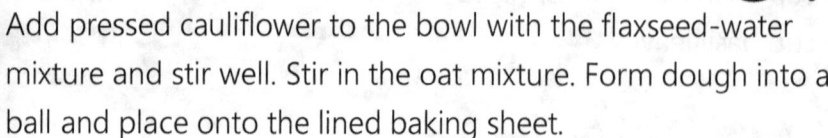
Add pressed cauliflower to the bowl with the flaxseed-water mixture and stir well. Stir in the oat mixture. Form dough into a ball and place onto the lined baking sheet.

6

Press dough ball down into a circle. Lay a sheet of parchment on top and roll dough flat using a rolling pin to about 1/4-inch thick.

7

Bake in the preheated oven until crust is set, about 15 minutes. Remove from the oven; leave oven on.

8

Place cashews into a pot with water to cover; bring to a boil. Reduce heat to medium-low and simmer until soft, about 15 minutes. Drain.

9

Puree boiled cashews, 1 1/4 cups fresh water, tapioca starch, nutritional yeast, cider vinegar, 1/2 teaspoon salt, and 1/4 teaspoon garlic powder in a blender. Pour puree into a saucepan over medium heat. Cook, stirring continuously, until thickened, about 5 minutes.

10

Heat olive oil in a saucepan over medium-high heat. Saute garlic until fragrant, about 2 minutes. Add crushed tomatoes, balsamic vinegar, maple syrup, 1 teaspoon salt, red pepper flakes, oregano, and black pepper. Simmer marinara sauce until flavors blend, about 10 minutes.

11

Fill blender halfway with marinara sauce. Cover and hold lid down with a potholder; pulse a few times before leaving on to blend. Pour into a bowl. Repeat with any remaining marinara sauce.

12

Spread marinara sauce over the cauliflower crust; top with the 'mozzarella cheese' and add cherry tomatoes.

13

Bake in the hot oven until sauce is bubbling and crust is golden brown, about 8 minutes. Top with basil.

NUTRITION FACTS:

339 calories; protein 11.4g; carbohydrates 37.4g; fat 18.9g;

SIMPLE VEGAN GARLICKY POTATOES

Prep:
20 mins
Cook:
20 mins
Total:
40 mins
Servings:
8
Yield:
8 servings

INGREDIENTS:

4 pounds potatoes, peeled and cut into chunks
4 cups water
2 cups vegetable broth
4 cloves garlic, thinly sliced, or more to taste
1 cup rice milk, or as needed

DIRECTIONS:

1

Combine potatoes, water, broth, and garlic in a pot. Bring to a boil; reduce heat to medium-low and cook until soft, about 15 minutes.

2

Drain potatoes and reserve cooking water. Return potatoes to the pot and stir over medium heat until any excess moisture is cooked off, about 1 minute.

3

Remove pot from heat. Add some reserved cooking water and rice milk, alternating between them, while stirring vigorously. Stop before potatoes become too soggy or liquid begins to accumulate in the pot.

NUTRITION FACTS:

203 calories; protein 5.3g; carbohydrates 44.9g; fat 0.6g;

JACKFRUIT VEGAN TACOS

Prep:
10 mins
Cook:
3 mins
Total:
13 mins
Servings:
4
Yield:
4 servings

INGREDIENTS:

2 (20 ounce) cans jackfruit in brine - drained, rinsed, and cut into bite-sized pieces
1 tablespoon vegetable oil
1 tablespoon water, or more as needed
2 tablespoons taco seasoning mix, or to taste
4 taco shells
½ cup salsa, or to taste

DIRECTIONS:

1

Heat oil in a small saucepan over medium heat. Add jackfruit; cook and stir for 2 to 3 minutes.
Add 1 tablespoon water and taco seasoning;
stir until well combined, about 1 minute.
Add additional water 1 tablespoon at a time as needed.

2

Place a small amount of jackfruit in each taco shell; add 2 tablespoons salsa.

NUTRITION FACTS:

258 calories; protein 1.6g; carbohydrates 27.8g; fat 13.3g;

VEGAN MUESLI

Prep:
10 mins
Additional:
8 hrs
Total:
8 hrs 10 mins
Servings:
6
Yield:
6 servings

INGREDIENTS:

2 cups rolled oats
1 ½ (14 ounce) cans coconut milk, or more to taste
3 tablespoons chia seeds
2 Granny Smith apples, peeled and grated
½ lemon, juiced
2 cups sliced strawberries
1 cup blueberries
2 tablespoons maple syrup, or to taste

DIRECTIONS:

1

Mix oats, coconut milk, and chia seeds together in a bowl.

2

Toss apples and lemon juice together in a bowl until coated; fold into oat mixture. Stir strawberries, blueberries, and maple syrup into oat mixture. Refrigerate for 8 hours to overnight.

NUTRITION FACTS:

392 calories; protein 7.1g; carbohydrates 42.2g; fat 24.6g; sodium 17.5mg.

VEGAN GRAVY

Prep:
5 mins
Cook:
10 mins
Total:
15 mins
Servings:
4
Yield:
4 servings

INGREDIENTS:

¼ cup canola oil
⅓ cup all-purpose flour
¼ cup vegetable broth
3 tablespoons tamari sauce
2 cups soy milk
2 tablespoons nutritional yeast
ground black pepper to taste

DIRECTIONS:

1

Heat oil in a skillet over medium heat. Whisk flour, vegetable broth, and tamari into hot oil; cook and stir until there are no lumps and the mixture becomes paste-like, about 5 minutes. Pour soy milk into the skillet; cook and stir until the mixture thickens, about 5 minutes more. Add yeast and black pepper; stir.

NUTRITION FACTS:

250 calories; protein 8.6g; carbohydrates 18.1g; fat 16.4g; sodium 846.4mg;

VEGAN POTATOES AU GRATIN

Prep:
20 mins
Cook:
25 mins
Total:
45 mins

INGREDIENTS:

6 large potatoes, peeled and cubed
1 ¼ cups vegetable broth, divided
2 tablespoons all-purpose flour
1 teaspoon seasoning salt
½ teaspoon ground black pepper
¼ teaspoon dry mustard
⅛ teaspoon nutmeg
2 cups soy milk
1 ½ cups shredded Cheddar-flavored soy cheese, divided
1 cup soft bread crumbs
3 teaspoons paprika

DIRECTIONS:

1

Preheat oven to 350 degrees F (175 degrees C).

2

Bring a large pot of salted water to a boil. Add potatoes and cook until tender but still firm, about 15 minutes. Drain and place in a 9 x 13 inch baking dish.

3

Meanwhile, in a small saucepan over high heat, boil 2 tablespoons of broth. Reduce heat to low. Stir in flour, seasoning salt, pepper, mustard and nutmeg. Gradually add soy milk, stirring constantly until thickened. Stir in half of the soy cheese. Stir constantly until cheese is melted. Pour over potatoes.

4

In a small bowl combine the remaining broth and the bread crumbs. Spoon evenly over potatoes.
Top with remaining soy cheese. Sprinkle with paprika.

5

Bake in preheated oven for 20 minutes.

NUTRITION FACTS:

322 calories; protein 9.2g; carbohydrates 66.9g; fat 2.6g; sodium 329.2mg

VEGAN QUINOA AND GUAC BOWL

Prep:
15 mins
Cook:
30 mins
Additional:
10 mins
Total:
55 mins
Servings:
4
Yield:
4 bowls

INGREDIENTS:

1 (15 ounce) can pinto beans, rinsed and drained

Quinoa:
2 ½ cups water
2 cups quinoa
½ teaspoon kosher salt

Veggie Bowl:

1 tablespoon olive oil
1 red bell pepper, sliced
1 yellow bell pepper, sliced
½ teaspoon ground black pepper
4 cups lettuce leaves
1 cup vegan shredded cheese blend
1 avocado - peeled, pitted, and sliced
¼ cup vegan sour cream

DIRECTIONS:

1

Heat pinto beans in a saucepan over low heat until hot, 5 to 7 minutes.

2

Bring water, quinoa, and salt to a boil in a saucepan and simmer until quinoa is tender and water is absorbed, 15 to 20 minutes. Remove from heat and set aside to cool, about 10 minutes.

3

Heat olive oil in a skillet over medium heat. Add red bell pepper, yellow bell pepper, and black pepper; cook and stir until bell peppers are softened but still crisp, about 10 minutes.

4

Toss quinoa, pinto beans, and lettuce together in a bowl. Top with pepper mixture, vegan cheese, avocado, and vegan sour cream.

NUTRITION FACTS:

623 calories; protein 24.6g; carbohydrates 78.2g; fat 23.5g; sodium 846.2mg

VEGAN STEW

Prep:
15 mins
Cook:
30 mins
Total:
45 mins
Servings:
4
Yield:
4 servings

INGREDIENTS:

1 onion, chopped
3 carrots, chopped
3 potatoes, chopped
1 parsnip, chopped
1 turnip, chopped
¼ cup uncooked white rice
1 teaspoon ground black pepper
1 teaspoon ground cumin
1 teaspoon salt
2 ½ cups water

DIRECTIONS:

1

In a large pot over medium-high heat, combine onion, carrots, potatoes, parsnip, turnip, rice, pepper, cumin, salt and water.
Boil until vegetables are tender, about 30 minutes, adding more water if necessary.

NUTRITION FACTS:

232 calories; protein 5.2g; carbohydrates 53g; fat 0.6g;

VEGAN FRENCH ONION SOUP

Prep:
15 mins
Cook:
1 hr 15 mins
Total:
1 hr 30 mins

INGREDIENTS:

Original recipe yields 6 servings
Ingredient Checklist
2 tablespoons buttery spread
1 tablespoon vegetable oil
3 pounds onions, halved and thinly sliced
3 cloves garlic, minced
½ teaspoon salt
2 tablespoons all-purpose flour
6 cups low-sodium vegetable broth
⅓ cup dry sherry
1 teaspoon Dijon mustard
1 teaspoon sherry vinegar
6 slices sourdough bread, toasted
⅔ cup shredded vegan cheese

DIRECTIONS:

1

Heat buttery spread and oil in a large, heavy saucepan over medium heat. Add onions, garlic, and salt.
Cook for 5 minutes, stirring often.
Reduce heat to very low and cook,
stirring occasionally,
until onions are very tender and brown, 50 to 60 minutes.

2

Add flour and cook, stirring constantly, for 3 to 4 minutes. Blend in broth, sherry, and Dijon mustard. Cover and simmer, stirring occasionally, for 15 minutes. Stir in sherry vinegar.

3

Set an oven rack about 6 inches from the heat source and preheat the oven's broiler. Ladle soup into 6 oven-proof bowls. Top each bowl with a slice of toast and some vegan cheese. Broil until cheesy is bubbly and golden, 1 to 2 minutes. Serve hot.

NUTRITION FACTS:

300 calories; protein 7.1g; carbohydrates 46.1g; fat 9.3g; sodium 888.3mg.

VEGAN SPRING ROLLS

Prep:
1 hr
Cook:
15 mins
Additional:
10 mins
Total:
1 hr 25 mins
Servings:
12
Yield:
12 servings

INGREDIENTS:

⅓ head cabbage, chopped
3 carrots, cut into matchstick-size pieces
1 cup finely chopped broccoli
2 tablespoons vegetable oil, or as needed, divided
1 onion, diced
1 cup chopped mushrooms
1 cup torn spinach

4 tablespoons liquid aminos

1 tablespoon hoisin sauce

12 ounces rice paper sheets

DIRECTIONS:

1

Place a steamer insert into a saucepan and fill with water to just below the bottom of the steamer.
Bring water to a boil.
Add cabbage, carrots, and broccoli, cover,
and steam until tender, 2 to 6 minutes.

2

While vegetables are steaming, heat 1 tablespoon oil in a large skillet over medium heat. Add onion; cook and stir 2 to 3 minutes. Add mushrooms and cook about 5 minutes more. Mix steamed vegetables into the skillet; add spinach, aminos, and hoisin sauce. Cook filling until spinach is limp, about 1 minute.

3

Fill a bowl the size of a rice paper sheet halfway with water.
Soak 1 sheet at a time until just softened. Place rice paper sheet on a clean work surface. Spoon 2 to 4 tablespoons of filling onto the middle of the sheet and roll the bottom up half-way.
Fold sides in, burrito-style, and continue rolling up snug.
Place filled roll on a plate.
Repeat with remaining
rice paper sheets and filling.

Set rolls in the refrigerator for 5 minutes; flip over and refrigerate until dry, about 5 minutes more.

4

Preheat the oven to 200 degrees F (95 degrees C).

5

Heat remaining 1 tablespoon oil in a skillet over medium heat. Fry rolls on each side,
turning periodically
to prevent over-browning, until
the rolls are a delicate golden color all over, 3 to 5 minutes. Place fried rolls on a baking sheet in the oven to keep hot until ready to serve.

NUTRITION FACTS:

46 calories; protein 1.8g; carbohydrates 5.8g; fat 2.5g; sodium 263.1mg

VEGAN MUSHROOM AND KALE SOUP

Prep:
20 mins
Cook:
30 mins
Total:
50 mins

INGREDIENTS:

1 tablespoon olive oil, or more to taste
2 russet potatoes, diced
2 carrots, diced, or more to taste
3 stalks celery, diced
1 onion, diced
1 ½ (32 fluid ounce) containers vegetable broth
2 (8 ounce) packages sliced mushrooms, divided
2 teaspoons salt
2 teaspoons herbes de Provence
1 teaspoon ground black pepper
1 bay leaf
2 cups chopped kale

DIRECTIONS:

1

Heat olive oil in a large saucepan over medium heat. Add potatoes, carrots, celery, and onion.
Cook and stir until fragrant, 3 to 5 minutes.
Add broth, 1 package of mushrooms,
salt, herbes de Provence, pepper, and bay leaf. Cook until vegetables are soft, 15 to 20 minutes.

2

Place kale in a separate saucepan over low heat and add water to cover. Cook until tender, 5 to 8 minutes. Drain excess liquid.

3

Coarsely chop the second package of mushrooms.

4

Fill blender halfway with the vegetables and broth. Cover and hold lid down with a potholder; pulse a few times before leaving on to blend. Pour into a pot. Repeat with remaining vegetables and broth.
Pour all of the pureed soup back into the saucepan. Add the kale and chopped mushrooms.
Let simmer until mushrooms are just tender, 5 to 10 minutes more.

DIRECTIONS:

230 calories; protein 9.1g; carbohydrates 40.4g; fat 5g; sodium 1929.4mg.

VEGAN COCONUT CURRY WITH TOFU

Prep:
15 mins
Cook:
20 mins
Total:
35 mins

INGREDIENTS:

¾ (16 ounce) package dried rice noodles
½ (16 ounce) package firm tofu, cut into small cubes
3 tablespoons cornstarch
3 tablespoons vegetable oil
1 teaspoon vegetable oil
1 tablespoon green curry paste
1 teaspoon minced garlic
1 teaspoon minced fresh ginger root
2 cups low-sodium vegetable broth
1 (14 ounce) can light coconut milk
2 green onions, finely chopped

DIRECTIONS:

1

Place noodles in a large bowl and cover with hot water. Set aside until noodles are softened, about 15 minutes. Drain and rinse thoroughly.

2

Roll tofu in cornstarch. Heat 3 tablespoons oil in a pan over medium-high heat. Fry tofu until crisp, about 5 minutes.

3

Combine 1 teaspoon oil, curry paste, garlic, and ginger in another pan over medium heat. Cook and stir until fragrant, about 2 minutes. Add vegetable broth and coconut milk slowly. Cook, stirring often, until sauce is heated through, about 10 minutes.

4

Combine noodles, tofu, curry sauce, and green onion in each serving bowl.

NUTRITION FACTS:

577 calories; protein 9.9g; carbohydrates 82g; fat 25.1g; sodium 344.6mg.

VEGAN PUMPKIN BREAD

Prep:
15 mins
Cook:
1 hr 5 mins
Additional:
15 mins
Total:
1 hr 35 mins
Servings:
20
Yield:
2 9x5-inch loaves

INGREDIENTS:

9 tablespoons water
3 tablespoons flaxseed meal
cooking spray
2 cups white sugar
¾ cup avocado oil
1 (16 ounce) can solid pack pumpkin puree
½ cup unsweetened applesauce
1 tablespoon molasses
1 teaspoon vanilla extract
1½ cups all-purpose flour

1 ½ cups whole wheat flour
1 ½ teaspoons ground cinnamon
1 teaspoon baking soda
½ teaspoon salt
½ teaspoon baking powder
½ teaspoon ground nutmeg
¼ teaspoon ground cloves

DIRECTIONS:

1

Stir water and flaxseed meal together in a small bowl until well combined. Place in the refrigerator until flax "eggs" have thickened, about 15 minutes.

2

Preheat the oven to 325 degrees F (165 degrees C). Spray two 9x5-inch loaf pans with cooking spray.

3

Combine sugar and avocado oil in a large bowl; beat with an electric mixer until blended. Mix in flax "eggs," pumpkin puree, applesauce, molasses, and vanilla extract.

4

Sift all-purpose flour, whole wheat flour, cinnamon, baking soda, salt, baking powder, nutmeg, and cloves together in a separate bowl. Add dry ingredients to the wet ingredients in 2 batches, stirring to combine after each addition.
Divide batter between the prepared loaf pans.

5

Bake in the preheated oven until a toothpick inserted into the center comes out clean, about 1 hour 5 minutes.

NUTRITION FACTS:

235 calories; protein 2.7g; carbohydrates 37.5g; fat 9g; sodium 189.8mg.

VEGAN SWEET AND SOUR MEATBALLS

Prep:
25 mins
Cook:
35 mins
Total:
60 mins
Servings:
4
Yield:
4 servings

INGREDIENTS:

½ cup warm water
2 tablespoons egg replacer
1 cup shredded vegan cheese
½ cup grated tofu
¼ cup nutritional yeast
1 teaspoon salt
½ teaspoon garlic powder
½ cup finely chopped onion
½ cup finely chopped pecans
1 tablespoon Italian seasoning

1 teaspoon dried basil

½ teaspoon dried sage

1 cup dry bread crumbs, or more as needed

Sauce:

¾ cup grape jelly

½ cup ketchup

¼ cup olive oil

¼ cup white vinegar

1 tablespoon chopped garlic

1 teaspoon dried oregano

DIRECTIONS:

1

Preheat oven to 350 degrees F (175 degrees C).

2

Mix warm water and egg replacer together in a large bowl. Stir in vegan cheese, tofu, nutritional yeast, salt, and garlic powder. Add onion, pecans, Italian seasoning, basil, and sage; mix until well combined. Stir in enough bread crumbs to reach a moist crumbly texture.

3

Form mixture into 1 1/2-inch balls and place in an 8-inch baking pan.

4

Mix grape jelly, ketchup, olive oil, vinegar, garlic, and oregano in a separate bowl. Pour over meatballs.

5

Bake in the preheated oven until meatballs are firm, 35 to 40 minutes.

NUTRITION FACTS:

703 calories; protein 15.6g; carbohydrates 84.5g; fat 35.1g

PROTEIN-PACKED VEGAN PANCAKES

Prep:
10 mins
Cook:
25 mins
Total:
35 mins
Servings:
6

INGREDIENTS:

1 cup ice cold water
4 tablespoons dry vegan egg replacer
1 cup all-purpose flour
1 cup blanched almond flour
4 tablespoons flax seed meal
2 tablespoons white sugar
2 teaspoons baking powder
1 teaspoon baking soda
2 cups almond milk
5 tablespoons vegan butter, or more as needed, divided
2 teaspoons vanilla extract

DIRECTIONS:

1

Combine ice cold water and vegan egg replacer in a large bowl; beat with an electric mixer until thick.

2

Stir together all-purpose flour, almond flour, flax seed meal, sugar, baking powder, and baking soda in a second bowl until well combined. Beat almond milk, 4 tablespoons vegan butter, and vanilla extract in a third bowl. Add flour mixture and almond milk mixture alternately to the vegan egg mixture, with blender set on medium speed.

3

Melt 1 tablespoon vegan butter in a skillet over medium heat. Pour 1/2 cup pancake batter into the pan; cook until bubbles form on the top and batter is set on the bottom, 2 to 3 minutes. Flip pancake and cook until light brown on the other side, about 2 minutes. Repeat with remaining batter, adding more vegan butter as necessary.

NUTRITION FACTS:

368 calories; protein 7.8g; carbohydrates 34.6g; fat 22.5g;

VEGAN BAKED POLENTA WITH RADICCHIO

Prep:
20 mins
Cook:
45 mins
Additional:
5 mins
Total:
70 mins
Servings:
6
Yield:
6 servings

INGREDIENTS:

3 teaspoons olive oil, divided
1 ½ cups vegetable broth
1 ½ cups water, divided
¾ cup unsweetened oat milk
1 ½ cups medium grind, whole-grain cornmeal
½ cup sliced yellow onion
½ cup shredded carrot
1 medium head radicchio, cored and thinly sliced

½ teaspoon coarse ground black pepper
½ teaspoon ground turmeric
3 (1 ounce) slices vegan smoked Gouda
3 ½ ounces vegan shredded mozzarella

DIRECTIONS:

1

Preheat the oven to 355 degrees F (180 degrees C). Grease an 8x8-inch baking pan with 1 teaspoon olive oil.

2

Combine vegetable broth and 1 cup water in a large pot and bring to a boil over high heat. Reduce heat to medium and keep at a low boil. Pour in unsweetened oat milk and bring to a boil. Sprinkle in cornmeal, whisking constantly to avoid clumps from forming. Reduce heat to medium-low and continue stirring until polenta begins to thicken. Add more water if needed. Stir until polenta has softened and thickened, about 20 minutes.

3

Meanwhile, heat remaining 2 teaspoons olive oil in a skillet. Add onion and carrot. Saute until vegetables have just begun to soften. Add radicchio and saute until wilted. Season with pepper and turmeric. Cook until vegetables are tender and cooked throughout, about 5 minutes.

4

Spread out 1/2 of the polenta in the greased baking dish. Evenly layer 1/2 of the vegan Gouda and 1/2 of the vegan mozzarella on top. Top with 1/2 of the radicchio mixture. Repeat layers with remaining polenta, cheeses, and radicchio mixture.

5

Bake in the preheated oven until cheese has melted and is bubbling, about 20 minutes. Allow to rest for 5 minutes before serving.

NUTRITION FACTS:

239 calories; protein 5.4g; carbohydrates 36.1g; fat 10.7g; sodium 492.9mg.

VEGAN APPLE DUMPLINGS

Prep:
45 mins
Cook:
25 mins
Total:
70 mins
Servings:
10
Yield:
10 dumplings

INGREDIENTS:

Dough:

2 cups all-purpose flour
4 tablespoons vegan margarine (such as Earth Balance®)
2 ½ teaspoons baking powder
1 teaspoon salt
1 cup water

Apple Marinade:

2 yellow apples, peeled and sliced into eighths
½ cup brown sugar
½ cup water
4 tablespoons vegan margarine melted
1 teaspoon vanilla extract
1 teaspoon ground cinnamon

DIRECTIONS:

1

Whisk flour, vegan margarine, baking powder, and salt together in a bowl until fine crumbs form. Add water and mix to combine. Separate dough into 10 equal pieces.

2

Preheat the oven to 350 degrees F (175 degrees C). Grease a baking sheet.

3

Chop each apple eighth into 4 chunks.
Place apple chunks in a saucepan and bring to a boil.
Cook until soft but not mushy, about 5 minutes.
Set aside to cool.

4

Combine brown sugar, water, vegan margarine, vanilla extract, and cinnamon in a microwave-safe bowl. Heat in the microwave until butter has dissolved, about 30 seconds. Stir marinade and pour over cooked apples in the saucepan.
Let apples marinate for 10 minutes.

5

Flatten a piece of dough into a circle. Place 4 apple chunks in the center and wrap dough around; pinch to seal. Place on the prepared baking sheet. Repeat with remaining dough and apples; reserve remaining marinade.

6

Drizzle remaining marinade over dumplings on the baking sheet.

7

Bake in the preheated oven until golden brown, 15 to 30 minutes. Serve hot.

NUTRITION FACTS:

227 calories; protein 2.7g; carbohydrates 33.8g; fat 9g;

GRILLABLE VEGAN BURGER

Prep:
25 mins
Cook:
20 mins
Total:
45 mins
Servings:
10
Yield:
10 burgers

INGREDIENTS:

2 cups raw walnuts
2 tablespoons olive oil
1 onion, minced
salt and ground black pepper to taste
3 cups rinsed and drained canned black beans
2 cups cooked rice
¾ cup vegan barbeque sauce
⅔ cup cornflake crumbs
2 tablespoons brown sugar
2 tablespoons chile powder

2 tablespoons ground paprika
2 tablespoons ground cumin

DIRECTIONS:

1

Toast walnuts in a skillet over medium heat, stirring frequently until lightly browned and fragrant, 5 to 7 minutes. Crush into fine pieces using a mortar and pestle or food processor.

2

Heat olive oil in the same skillet over medium heat. Cook and stir onion until lightly browned, about 5 minutes. Season with salt and pepper.

3

Mash black beans in a large bowl using a fork. Add walnuts, onion, rice, barbeque sauce, cornflake crumbs, brown sugar, chile powder, paprika, and cumin. Season with salt and pepper; stir until mixture is well combined and holds together. Shape into 10 burgers.

4

Preheat an outdoor grill for medium heat and lightly oil the grate. Place burgers on aluminum foil and grill until browned, 5 to 8 minutes per side.

NUTRITION FACTS:

444 calories; protein 11.6g; carbohydrates 58.6g; fat 19.6g; sodium 725.5mg.

VEGAN LASAGNA

Prep:
30 mins
Cook:
2 hrs
Total:
2 hrs 30 mins
Servings:
8
Yield:
8 servings

INGREDIENTS:

2 tablespoons olive oil
1 ½ cups chopped onion
3 tablespoons minced garlic
4 (14.5 ounce) cans stewed tomatoes
⅓ cup tomato paste
½ cup chopped fresh basil
½ cup chopped parsley
1 teaspoon salt
1 teaspoon ground black pepper
1 (16 ounce) package lasagna noodles
2 pounds firm tofu
2 tablespoons minced garlic

¼ cup chopped fresh basil
¼ cup chopped parsley
½ teaspoon salt
ground black pepper to taste
3 (10 ounce) packages frozen chopped spinach, thawed and drained

DIRECTIONS:

1

Make the sauce: In a large, heavy saucepan, over medium heat, heat the olive oil. Place the onions in the saucepan and saute them until they are soft, about 5 minutes. Add the garlic; cook 5 minutes more.

2

Place the tomatoes, tomato paste, basil and parsley in the saucepan. Stir well, turn the heat to low and let the sauce simmer covered for 1 hour. Add the salt and pepper.

3

While the sauce is cooking bring a large kettle of salted water to a boil. Boil the lasagna noodles for 9 minutes, then drain and rinse well.

4

Preheat the oven to 400 degrees F (200 degrees C).

5

Place the tofu blocks in a large bowl. Add the garlic, basil and parsley. Add the salt and pepper, and mash all the ingredients together by squeezing pieces of tofu through your fingers. Mix well.

6

Assemble the lasagna: Spread 1 cup of the tomato sauce in the bottom of a 9x13 inch casserole pan. Arrange a single layer of lasagna noodles, sprinkle one-third of the tofu mixture over the noodles. Distribute the spinach evenly over the tofu. Next ladle 1 1/2 cups tomato sauce over the tofu, and top it with another layer of the noodles. Then sprinkle another 1/3 of the tofu mixture over the noodles, top the tofu with 1 1/2 cups tomato sauce, and place a final layer of noodles over the tomato sauce. Finally, top the noodles with the final 1/3 of the tofu, and spread the remaining tomato sauce over everything.

7

Cover the pan with foil and bake the lasagna for 30 minutes. Serve hot and enjoy.

NUTRITION FACTS:

511 calories; protein 32.5g; carbohydrates 69.9g; fat 15.8g;

VEGAN CURRIED CAULIFLOWER, SWEET POTATO, AND LENTIL SOUP

Prep:
20 mins
Cook:
50 mins
Total:
70 mins
Servings:
5
Yield:
5 servings

INGREDIENTS:

1 tablespoon coconut oil
1 large onion, chopped
4 cloves garlic, minced
1 tablespoon minced fresh ginger, or more to taste
1 tablespoon curry powder, or more to taste
2 teaspoons ground coriander

2 teaspoons ground cumin

8 cups vegetable broth

1 cup dry red lentils, rinsed and drained

1 head cauliflower, broken into florets

2 cups cubed sweet potato

3 cups fresh spinach

DIRECTIONS:

1

Heat coconut oil in a large saucepan over medium heat. Add onion and garlic and saute until translucent, 5 to 6 minutes. Stir in ginger, 1 tablespoon curry powder, coriander, and cumin and saute until fragrant, about 2 minutes more. Pour in broth and lentils and stir to combine. Bring mixture to a low boil; reduce heat and simmer for 5 minutes.

2

Stir in cauliflower and sweet potato. Cover, reduce heat to medium-low, and simmer until cauliflower and sweet potato are tender, 20 to 25 minutes. Season with salt and pepper and add more curry powder if desired. Stir in spinach and cook until wilted, 3 to 5 minutes.

NUTRITION FACTS:

313 calories; protein 16.1g; carbohydrates 53.9g; fat 4.7g; sodium 820.3mg.

VEGAN ITALIAN VEGETABLE SOUP

Servings:
6
Yield:
6 servings

INGREDIENTS:

2 (14.5 ounce) cans vegetable broth
1 (28 ounce) can peeled and crushed tomatoes
2 large carrots, coarsely chopped
½ cup frozen green beans
1 stalk celery, thickly sliced
⅓ cup frozen pearl onions
2 cloves garlic, minced
1 tablespoon dried parsley
¾ teaspoon dried basil
1 bay leaf
1 cube vegetable bouillon
½ cup macaroni
1 (15 ounce) can kidney beans, drained
3 small zucchinis, cubed

DIRECTIONS:

1

In large saucepan or Dutch oven, bring broth, tomatoes, carrots, frozen green beans, celery, onions, garlic, parsley, basil, bay leaf and vegetable bouillon cube to a boil. Reduce heat. Cover and simmer 15 minutes.

2

Stir in macaroni, kidney beans, and zucchini. Bring soup back to a boil, and then reduce heat to simmer. Cover and cook for 10 to 15 minutes. Remove bay leaf and serve.

NUTRITION FACTS:

185 calories; protein 9.1g; carbohydrates 37.2g; fat 1.3g; sodium 634.4mg.

VEGAN SWEET POTATO CHICKPEA CURRY

Prep:
10 mins
Cook:
20 mins
Total:
30 mins
Servings:
6
Yield:
6 servings

INGREDIENTS:

3 tablespoons olive oil
1 onion, chopped
2 cloves garlic, minced
2 teaspoons minced fresh ginger root
1 (15 ounce) can chickpeas, drained
1 (14.5 ounce) can diced tomatoes
1 (14 ounce) can coconut milk
1 sweet potato, cubed
1 tablespoon garam masala
1 teaspoon ground cumin

1 teaspoon ground turmeric
½ teaspoon salt
¼ teaspoon red chile flakes
1 cup baby spinach

DIRECTIONS:

1

Heat oil in a skillet over medium heat and cook onion, garlic, and ginger until softened, about 5 minutes. Add chickpeas, tomatoes, coconut milk, and sweet potato. Bring to a boil, reduce heat to low and simmer until tender, about 15 minutes.

2

Season with garam masala, cumin, turmeric, chile flakes, and salt. Add spinach right before serving.

NUTRITION FACTS:

293 calories; protein 5.1g; carbohydrates 22.3g; fat 21.6g; sodium 515mg;

VEGAN BURRITOS

Prep:
30 mins
Cook:
55 mins
Total:
85 mins
Servings:
6
Yield:
6 burritos

INGREDIENTS:

2 ¼ cups water
1 cup uncooked brown rice
1 (10 ounce) can diced tomatoes and green chiles
3 teaspoons ground cumin
2 teaspoons ground turmeric
1 teaspoon chopped fresh basil
1 pinch garlic powder, or to taste
1 pinch salt and ground black pepper to taste
1 pinch seasoned salt, or to taste
2 tablespoons olive oil
2 large red potatoes, cubed
1 green bell pepper, chopped

1 medium onion, chopped
1 clove garlic, minced, or to taste
1 (15 ounce) can black beans, rinsed and drained
6 flour tortillas
1 cup fresh spinach, or to taste
1 cup chopped romaine lettuce, or to taste
¼ cup salsa, or to taste

DIRECTIONS:

1

Preheat the oven to 350 degrees F (175 degrees C). Grease a baking sheet.

2

Bring water and brown rice to a boil in a saucepan. Stir in diced tomatoes with chile peppers. Reduce heat to medium-low, cover, and simmer until rice is tender and liquid has been absorbed, about 50 minutes.

3

While rice is cooking, mix cumin, turmeric, basil, garlic powder, salt, pepper, and seasoned salt together in a large bowl. Add olive oil. Toss potatoes in the mixture until well coated. Lay potatoes in a single layer on the prepared baking sheet.

4

Bake in the preheated oven until fork-tender, 15 to 30 minutes, depending on the size of the cubes, checking halfway through cooking time and flipping over as needed.

5

While potatoes are cooking, heat a skillet over medium heat. Saute bell pepper and onion in the hot pan until softened, about 5 minutes. Add garlic and cook for 1 minute. Remove from heat and set aside.

6

Heat black beans in a saucepan over medium-low heat until hot, 2 to 3 minutes. Keep warm.

7

Meanwhile, heat tortillas in a separate skillet over low heat until warm, 1 to 2 minutes, or according to package instructions.

8

Lay out tortillas and fill as desired with cooked rice, beans, potatoes, pepper-onion mixture, spinach, romaine lettuce, and salsa as desired.
Wrap up into burritos and serve.

NUTRITION FACTS:

495 calories; protein 14.6g; carbohydrates 89.3g; fat 9.7g; sodium 841.4mg.

VEGAN PUMPKIN COOKIES

Prep:
10 mins
Cook:
10 mins
Additional:
10 mins
Total:
30 mins
Servings:
20
Yield:
20 cookies

INGREDIENTS:

2 cups all-purpose flour
1 (15 ounce) can pumpkin puree
1 ⅓ cups white sugar
⅓ cup vanilla-flavored almond milk
¼ cup vegetable oil
1 teaspoon baking soda
1 teaspoon ground cinnamon
1 teaspoon vanilla extract

½ teaspoon salt

½ teaspoon cinnamon sugar

DIRECTIONS:

1

Preheat oven to 400 degrees F (200 degrees C).

2

Combine flour, pumpkin, sugar, almond milk, vegetable oil, baking soda, cinnamon, vanilla extract, salt, and cinnamon sugar in a bowl until dough is smooth. Spoon dough, about 1 tablespoon per cookie, onto baking sheet.

3

Bake in the preheated oven until edges of cookies are beginning to crisp along the edges, 10 to 12 minutes. Cool cookies on baking sheet for 2 minutes before transferring to a wire rack to cool completely.

NUTRITION FACTS:

131 calories; protein 1.5g; carbohydrates 25.1g; fat 3g; sodium 175.4mg.

VEGAN PORTOBELLO STROGANOFF

Prep:
10 mins
Cook:
40 mins
Additional:
20 mins
Total:
70 mins
Servings:
4
Yield:
4 servings

INGREDIENTS:

8 ounces vegan sour cream (such as Tofutti®)
½ cup water (Optional)
3 tablespoons dried minced onion
2 tablespoons all-purpose flour
2 teaspoons vegan no-beef bouillon
¼ teaspoon garlic powder
¼ teaspoon dried basil
¼ teaspoon ground black pepper

½ cup dry red wine
1 tablespoon olive oil
2 tablespoons soy sauce
1 tablespoon balsamic vinegar
2 cloves garlic, minced
2 large portobello mushroom caps, stems and gills removed
cooking spray
¼ cup water, or as needed (Optional)

DIRECTIONS:

1

Whisk vegan sour cream, 1/2 cup water, minced onion, flour, vegan bouillon, garlic powder, basil, and black pepper in a bowl. Cover and refrigerate.

2

Preheat oven to 400 degrees F (200 degrees C).

3

Whisk red wine, olive oil, soy sauce, balsamic vinegar, and garlic in another bowl.

4

Arrange mushroom caps with gill sides up in a baking dish and pour red wine mixture on top. Marinate for 20 minutes, then cover baking dish with aluminum foil.

5

Bake mushrooms in the preheated oven for 30 minutes. Remove foil, flip mushrooms, and continue baking until very tender, about 10 minutes more. Set aside to cool; dice mushrooms.

6

Heat a saucepan sprayed with cooking spray over medium heat. Cook and stir mushrooms in sauce pan until lightly browned, about 5 minutes; reduce heat to low.

7

Stir sour cream sauce into mushrooms. Continue to cook and stir until thickened, 1 to 2 minutes more. If the sauce becomes too thick, stir in 1/4 cup water.

NUTRITION FACTS:

259 calories; protein 3.3g; carbohydrates 25.9g; fat 13.5g; sodium 778.2mg

VEGAN MUSHROOM RISOTTO

Prep:
15 mins
Cook:
45 mins
Total:
60 mins
Servings:
4
Yield:
4 servings

INGREDIENTS:

6 cups vegetable stock, or more if needed
4 tablespoons olive oil, divided
2 (8 ounce) packages baby bella mushrooms, chopped
1 medium onion, diced
1 celery stalk, diced
3 cloves garlic, minced
2 cups Arborio rice
1 cup dry white wine
1 ½ teaspoons dried thyme
½ teaspoon salt, or to taste

½ teaspoon freshly cracked black pepper, or to taste

DIRECTIONS:

1

Pour vegetable stock into a large pot and bring to a boil over
medium heat. Reduce heat to low, cover,
and keep warm.

2

Heat 2 tablespoons olive oil in a large Dutch oven over medium-high heat. Add mushrooms and cook, stirring occasionally, until softened, about 10 minutes. Add onion and cook until soft and translucent, about 5 minutes. Stir in celery and garlic, and cook until garlic is fragrant, about 3 minutes.

3

Add remaining 2 tablespoons olive oil and Arborio rice to the pot. Cook, stirring often, until rice is opaque and smells slightly toasted, 2 to 4 minutes. Stir in white wine, and cook until it evaporates, an additional 2 to 3 minutes. Season with thyme, salt, and pepper.

4

Begin stirring in reserved warm vegetable stock,
1 cup at a time, allowing each addition
of stock to be fully absorbed before adding in the next, stirring continuously. Continue adding broth gradually while stirring

constantly, until rice is tender and creamy, about 20 minutes. Season with additional salt and pepper.

NUTRITION FACTS:

670 calories; protein 12.7g; carbohydrates 110.5g; fat 14.6g;

EASY VEGAN WAFFLES

Prep:
10 mins
Cook:
40 mins
Total:
50 mins
Servings:
8
Yield:
8 waffles

INGREDIENTS:

4 tablespoons dry vegan egg replacer
½ cup ice cold water
1 ¾ cups almond milk
1 ¾ cups all-purpose flour
½ cup almond flour
½ cup vegetable oil
1 tablespoon baking powder
1 tablespoon white sugar
2 teaspoons vanilla extract
nonstick cooking spray

DIRECTIONS:

1

Preheat a waffle iron according to manufacturer's instructions.

2

Combine egg replacer and water in a blender; blend until smooth and all lumps have disappeared. Add almond milk, all-purpose flour, almond flour, oil, baking powder, sugar, and vanilla extract; blend on low until smooth.

3

Spray the preheated waffle iron with cooking spray. Pour batter by 1/4-cupfuls onto the iron and cook until waffle is golden brown and the iron stops steaming, about 5 minutes.

NUTRITION FACTS:

306 calories; protein 4.7g; carbohydrates 30.6g; fat 18.5g; sodium 223.9mg.

QUICK VEGAN EGGPLANT PASTA

Prep:
15 mins
Cook:
43 mins
Total:
58 mins
Servings:
4
Yield:
4 servings

INGREDIENTS:

1 (16 ounce) package spaghetti
3 tablespoons olive oil
2 large onions, finely chopped
2 large eggplants, cubed
1 clove garlic, pressed
2 (14.5 ounce) cans whole peeled tomatoes
1 tablespoon capers
coarse salt and ground black pepper to taste
3 tablespoons chopped fresh basil

DIRECTIONS:

1

Bring a large pot of lightly salted water to a boil. Cook spaghetti in the boiling water, stirring occasionally, until tender yet firm to the bite, about 12 minutes. Drain.

2

Heat olive oil in a nonstick skillet over medium-low heat and cook onions until soft and translucent, 3 to 5 minutes. Add eggplants and garlic and cook until softened, 3 to 5 minutes. Add tomatoes and capers; cook until eggplant is soft, about 20 minutes. Season with salt and pepper and stir in fresh basil.

3

Serve eggplant sauce over spaghetti.

NUTRITION FACTS:

653 calories; protein 20.6g; carbohydrates 118.6g; fat 12.8g; sodium 409.7mg.

VEGAN CHOCOLATE PIE

Prep:
5 mins
Cook:
10 mins
Additional:
2 hrs
Total:
2 hrs 15 mins
Servings:
8
Yield:
1 pie

INGREDIENTS:

2 cups almond milk
1 (5 ounce) package non-instant chocolate pudding mix
¼ cup vegan chocolate chips
1 vegan graham cracker crust
½ cup vegan whipped cream

DIRECTIONS:

1

Combine almond milk and pudding mix in a saucepan and bring to a boil, stirring constantly, over medium heat. As soon as pudding boils, reduce heat to low and continue cooking and stirring until pudding thickens, about 5 minutes.

2

Remove from heat and stir in chocolate chips until melted. Pour into graham crust and refrigerate until set, about 2 hours.

3

Top with vegan whipped cream

NUTRITION FACTS:

240 calories; protein 2.1g; carbohydrates 40.8g; fat 10.2g; sodium 277.6mg.

VEGAN SEITAN CURRY WITH RICE

Prep:
10 mins
Cook:
50 mins
Total:
60 mins

INGREDIENTS:

⅓ cup basmati rice
1 small zucchini, cubed
½ onion, cubed
4 ½ ounces seitan beef, sliced
1 teaspoon pure coconut oil
1 tablespoon cumin
1 tablespoon ground coriander
1 teaspoon curry powder
½ teaspoon salt
½ teaspoon ground turmeric
1 pinch ground black pepper
1 pinch garlic powder
⅔ cup water

DIRECTIONS:

1

Soak basmati rice in 1/2 cup cold water for 30 minutes. Drain.

2

Combine zucchini and onion in a pot of water, bring to a boil, and boil for about 20 minutes. Drain. Place in a blender; blend until smooth.

3

Pour pureed zucchini mixture into a pot over medium heat. Add seitan, coconut oil, cumin, coriander, curry powder, salt, turmeric, pepper, and garlic powder. Simmer until sauce is thick, adding a tablespoon of water from time to time to prevent burning, about 30 minutes.

4

Meanwhile, combine 2/3 cup water and soaked rice in a saucepan and bring to a boil. Reduce heat to medium-low, cover, and simmer until rice is tender and water has been absorbed, 20 to 25 minutes.

5

Serve seitan with hot rice.

NUTRITION FACTS:

547 calories; protein 36.3g; carbohydrates 80.8g; fat 10.8g; sodium 1600.2mg.

VEGAN BLUEBERRY MUFFINS WITH APPLESAUCE

Prep:
10 mins
Cook:
35 mins
Total:
45 mins
Servings:
12
Yield:
1 dozen muffins

INGREDIENTS:

1 cooking spray
2 cups fresh blueberries
2 cups all-purpose flour
1 cup lightly packed brown sugar
½ cup unsweetened applesauce
½ cup soy milk
¼ cup soy margarine
1 tablespoon baking powder

1 teaspoon vanilla extract
½ teaspoon salt

DIRECTIONS:

1

Preheat the oven to 350 degrees F (175 degrees C). Line 12 cups of a mini muffin tin with paper liners or spray with cooking spray.

2

Mix blueberries, flour, sugar, applesauce, soy milk, soy margarine, baking powder, vanilla extract, and salt together in a bowl. Spoon batter into muffin cups, filling them 3/4-full.

3

Bake in the preheated oven until tops are firm, about 35 minutes. Cool slightly on a rack.

NUTRITION FACTS:

205 calories; protein 2.7g; carbohydrates 39.6g; fat 4.2g; sodium 274mg.

VEGAN AFRICAN STEW

Prep:
15 mins
Cook:
1 hr 40 mins
Total:
1 hr 55 mins

INGREDIENTS:

2 tablespoons olive oil
3 cups chopped yams
2 large onions, chopped
2 cups chopped cabbage
2 tomatoes, chopped
6 tablespoons flaked coconut
3 cloves garlic, minced
3 cups tomato juice
1 cup apple juice
1 teaspoon ground ginger
¼ teaspoon cayenne pepper
1 pinch salt
1 large green bell pepper, chopped
½ cup peanut butter

DIRECTIONS:

1

Heat olive oil in a Dutch oven over medium-high heat. Cook and stir yams, onions, cabbage, tomatoes, coconut, and garlic in the hot oil until the vegetables are slightly browned, 7 to 10 minutes.

2

Pour tomato juice and apple juice into the Dutch oven; season with ginger, cayenne pepper, and salt. Reduce heat to medium-low and cook at a simmer for 1 hour.

3

Stir bell pepper and peanut butter into the mixture. Cook, stirring regularly, until the peanut butter is melted completely into the soup, about 30 minutes more.

NUTRITION FACTS:

379 calories; protein 9.6g; carbohydrates 46.8g; fat 19.6g; sodium 446.8mg.

VEGAN PUMPKIN PIE

Prep:
15 mins
Cook:
40 mins
Additional:
9 hrs
Total:
9 hrs 55 mins
Servings:
8
Yield:
1 pie

INGREDIENTS:

1 cup vanilla-flavored almond milk
½ cup raw sugar
2 tablespoons arrowroot powder
1 (15 ounce) can pumpkin puree
2 teaspoons pumpkin pie spice
½ teaspoon salt
1 (9 inch) vegan pie shell

DIRECTIONS:

1

Preheat oven to 375 degrees F (190 degrees C).

2

Combine almond milk, sugar, and arrowroot powder in a blender; blend until sugar and arrowroot are completely dissolved. Add pumpkin puree, pumpkin pie spice, and salt; blend until smooth. Pour into the pie shell. Cover edges of the pie shell with aluminum foil.

3

Bake in the preheated oven until center is set, about 40 minutes.

4

Cool pie to room temperature, about 1 hour. Refrigerate until firm, 8 hours to overnight.

NUTRITION FACTS:

202 calories; protein 2.2g; carbohydrates 30.8g; fat 8.3g;

ORANGE VEGAN CAKE

Prep:
15 mins
Cook:
30 mins
Total:
45 mins
Servings:
16
Yield:
1 8x8-inch pan

INGREDIENTS:

1 large orange, peeled
1 ½ cups all-purpose flour
1 cup white sugar
½ cup vegetable oil
1 ½ teaspoons baking soda
¼ teaspoon salt

DIRECTIONS:

1

Preheat oven to 375 degrees F (190 degrees C). Grease an 8x8-inch baking pan.

2

Blend orange in the blender until liquified; measure 1 cup orange juice.

3

Whisk orange juice, flour, sugar, vegetable oil, baking soda, and salt together in a bowl. Pour batter into the prepared pan.

4

Bake in the preheated oven until a toothpick inserted in the center of the cake comes out clean, about 30 minutes.

NUTRITION FACTS:

157 calories; protein 1.3g; carbohydrates 22.8g; fat 7g; sodium 154.6mg.

VEGAN DILLY RANCH

Prep:
5 mins
Additional:
1 hr
Total:
1 hr 5 mins
Servings:
12
Yield:
1 1/2 cups

INGREDIENTS:

1 ¼ cups cashew milk
¼ cup raw cashews
1 tablespoon fresh lemon juice
1 tablespoon chia seeds, or more to taste
1 teaspoon onion powder
¼ teaspoon salt
¼ teaspoon granulated garlic
1 tablespoon dried chopped onion
1 tablespoon dried dill
1 tablespoon dried parsley

DIRECTIONS:

1

Combine cashew milk, cashews, lemon juice, chia seeds, onion powder, salt, and granulated garlic in a blender.
Blend on high speed until smooth.
Add dried onion, dill, and parsley;
pulse a few times more.

2

Refrigerate until well chilled, at least 1 hour.

NUTRITION FACTS:

53 calories; protein 0.7g; carbohydrates 2.8g; fat 4.6g; sodium 143mg.

www.ingramcontent.com/pod-product-compliance
Lightning Source LLC
Chambersburg PA
CBHW070102120526
44589CB00033B/1517